ISBN-13: 978-1533175113

www.paladin-iinformation-assurance.com

First Printing, 2016. Second Printing, 2017

Printed in the United States of America

Liability Disclaimer

Disclaimer: The author of this report is an information security specialist, not an attorney. The opinions contained should not be construed as legal advice. The reader should consult with a licensed attorney if legal counsel is required relative to Florida Statute 501.171.

By reading this book, you assume all risks associated with using the advice given below, with a full understanding that you, solely, are responsible for anything that may occur as a result of putting this information into action in any way, and regardless of your interpretation of the advice.

You further agree that our company cannot be held responsible in any way for the success or failure of your business as a result of the information presented in this book. It is your responsibility to conduct your own due diligence regarding the safe and successful operation of your business if you intend to apply any of our information in any way to your business operations.

Florida's Information Protection Statute 501.171

Where Do You Stand?

Dr. William G. Perry

Foreword

We extensively use computers, networks and the Internet to conduct business today. They are fast, efficient and necessary. There is, however, a dark side.

Cyber criminals prowl the Internet looking for openings to exploit. They want to steal, alter, destroy or otherwise illicitly use the electronic information you possess.

Vulnerabilities and threats are growing. Law enforcement has been unable to stem the tide. Law-makers in Florida, however, have decided who should have the lion's share of the responsibility protecting "personally identifiable information" or PII. You.

Where do you stand? Are you generally aware of the provisions of the law? Is your information system resilient enough to block a cyber attack? Hopefully, your privately held confidential information is well-protected and you can meet the test of having provided "reasonable measures" to protect the confidential information that you possess on employees, customers and others. Otherwise you are exposed to a substantial risk.

This publication is designed to inform you about the basics of what you need to consider in order to be in compliance privacy with FS 501.171.

You will see, throughout this publication, a statement similar to the one below:

Disclaimer: The author of this report is an information security specialist, not an attorney. The opinions contained should not be construed as legal advice. The reader should consult with a licensed attorney if legal counsel is required relative to 501.171.

The author is a security analyst who is qualified to assess the robustness of an information security plan. As the disclaimer states, consult with a licensed attorney for any and all legal matters.

Dedication

To Frank Rodriguez for perseverance; to Shirley Perry for the gift of Faith and to John Peterson for a discipline

Table of Contents

Introduction 9

Definition of Terms 11

Requirements for Data Security 18

Notice to Department of Security Breach 21

Notice to Individuals of Security Breach 23

Notice to Credit Reporting Agencies 26

Notice by Third-Party Agents; Duties of Third Party
Agents Notice by Agents 26

Annual Report 27

Requirements for Disposal of Customer Records ... 28

Enforcement 28

No Private Cause for Action 29

Public Records Exemption 29

How Can You Improve Information Security and
Pevent Unauthorized Disclosures? 34

Summary 48

Florida's Information Protection Statute 501.171: Where Do You Stand?

William G. Perry, Ph.D.

Disclaimer: The author of this report is an information security specialist, not an attorney. The opinions contained in this report should not be construed as legal advice. The reader should consult with a licensed attorney if legal counsel is required relative to the above named Statute.

Introduction

Nearly everyone would agree that businesses and other organizations face cyber risks on a routine basis. You can't read a story in print, watch a national newscast or listen to the radio without hearing about the latest information security breaches originating from the Internet.

The problem is global. <u>Financial losses from cybercrime and the unlawful use of information now surpass the total of the illegal drug trade.</u> Cybercriminals can inflict irreparable harm on individuals, companies and national security. Law enforcement is way behind the curve in putting a stop to unauthorized access to private in-information.

Information security breaches are now set to become even worse. Here's why. The original number of Internet addresses was 4.2 billion. The new Internet addressing scheme will create 340 trillion, trillion addresses. That number, when written, appears as follows: 340,282,366,920,938,000,000,000,000,000,000,000,000. Each of these addresses is subject to malicious attack.

Internet enabled and embedded devices are now beginning to be used on factory floors, shops and thousands of consumer devices. The attack surface is expanding dramatically. Everyone who depends upon technology to conduct private and personal business is at risk.

Federal and state governments are becoming more aware of the threats and vulnerabilities and are making attempts to confront the problem. Florida passed its cyber security law as an effort to help protect against the unauthorized disclosure of private information in 2014. The Statute falls under Chapter 501, Consumer Protection Chapter and Section 171, Security of Confidential Personal Information.

Very few, if any, companies or organizations are exempt from the law. Virtually any entity doing business in Florida is now required to comply with the law.

Do you know what is required of you under FS 501.171? If not, you need to look at the law's major provisions.

Definition of Terms

"Breach of Security" or "breach" - Florida's confidential information law, among other things, was crafted to protect against the unauthorized access and use of private data.

Rightfully so, when employees of an organization access sensitive information in the course of fulfilling his or her job responsibilities, there hasn't been an unauthorized access or use of the private data. However, if an authorized employee accesses confidential private information and gives it to an unauthorized person, the law has been violated.

Let's consider a number of scenarios that illustrate:

a.) A receptionist in a medical center greets a patient who has an appointment with a physician. She asks for the patient's full name, accesses her computer and retrieves the patient's record. This act represents the authorized access of personal medical data. However, if the patient's record is clipped to the door in the hallway and another patient removes the file and takes it from the building, it is a clear example of data theft.

b.) Let's assume that an employee in a company's personnel department accesses the salary figures of each employee, makes a list of how much each person is paid and sends everyone in the organization a copy. That is a clear example of unauthorized use. The person who accessed the record may very well have had the authority to access employees' private information but was without the authority to publish it to everyone.

c.) Assume that a member of an organization's housekeeping staff notices one night that a computer has been left on. Curiosity gets the better of the individual. He or she takes a look at the confidential information on the screen and writes down as many employee names and social security numbers as possible with the idea of stealing his or her identity. This example would clearly be an act of unauthorized access and unauthorized use of the confidential information.

d.) A computer cracker intrudes upon a company's computer network and downloads the confidential information of customers. This is plainly an unauthorized access of data.

"Covered entity", according to FS 501.71, means a sole proprietorship, partnership, corporation, trust, estate, cooperative association or other commercial entity that acquires, maintains, stores, or uses personal information. Further, for the purpose of giving the required proper notice the term "covered entity" may include a governmental entity.

Finding an organization engaged in business and commerce or any other activity that fails to fall under the category of a "covered entity" would be difficult. One that comes to mind might be a street vendor who is only paid in cash for his or her products.

A person should consult with an attorney if wondering about the status of his or her business and if it is a "covered entity". The wise and prudent thing to do would be to assume that if you are acquiring or maintaining confidential personal data on people, you are likely considered to be a "covered entity".

"Customer records" is explained in the wording of the Statute as being any material, regardless of the physical form, on which personal information is recorded or preserved by any means, including, but not limited to, written or spoken words, graphically depicted, printed or electromagnetically transmitted that are provided by an individual in this state (Florida) to a covered entity for the purpose of purchasing or leasing a product or obtaining a service.

The scope of what is a customer record is quite broad. Virtually any information provided by an individual to a covered entity is subject to the Statute. Let's look at a number of examples:

a.) When a customer hands an employee of a covered entity his or her credit card the business is subject to the provisions of a statute.

b.) When an email is sent and it contains personal information it is considered to be a customer record.

c.) An electronic database that holds confidential information on individuals and is stored in a company database is considered to be a customer record.

d.) Information on people that is stored as a "hard copy" or on any type of disk drive is likely considered to be a customer record for the purpose of the Statute. When in doubt you are encouraged to consult with an attorney.

e.) The Statute would appear to even include the possibility of the spoken word being considered as a customer record. Care should be taken when discussing information related to any type of customer record.

f.) Scanning a document and removing it from a secure place or sending it to a third party would also be considered a "customer record".

"Data in electronic form" is a phrase that means any data that is stored on a digital device, or any computer system or database and includes recordable disks, smart phones and other mass storage devices. Data in an electronic form could be private information in a remote location or by a third party like an organization that provides back up storage for the covered entity. Let's consider a couple of examples:

a.) An organization that uses a cloud storage service has direct responsibility for complying with FS 501.171.

b.) Any laptops being used by a covered entity that stores private information would make such equipment and processes associated with it to be subject to the law.

c.) Another example might be the customer information that is stored on a company's mobile phones. Please consult with an attorney if you are in doubt.

*"**Department**"* is defined in the Statute as the Department of Legal Affairs in the Florida Attorney General's Office. The website may be accessed at: http://myfloridalegal.com.

*"**Government entity**"* means any of the following for the purpose of the Statute: any department, division, bureau, commission, regional planning agency, board, district, authority, agency, or other instrumentality of this State that acquires, maintains, stores, or uses data in electronic form containing personal information. Government agencies must comply with the reporting requirements as outlined in Florida's confidential information Statute 501.171 (3)-(6).

The above definition for a covered government entity indicates that virtually any State agency or instrumentality of the State is included in the provisions of the privacy law.

*"**Personal Information**"* means the following:

a.) An individual's first name or first initial and the last name in combination with any one or more of the following data elements:

  I.)   A social security number;

  II.) A driver license or identification card number, passport number, military identification number or other similar number issued on a government document used to verify identity;

III.) A financial account number or credit or debit card number, in combination with any required security code, access code, or password that is necessary to permit access to an individual's financial account;

IV.) Any information regarding an individual's medical history, mental or physical condition, or medical treatment or diagnosis by a health care professional; or

V.) An individual's health insurance policy number or subscriber identification number and any unique identifier used by a health insurer to identify the individuals.

b.) A user name or e-mail address, in combination with a password or security question, would permit access to an online account.

The term, *"personal information"* does not include information on an individual that has been made publicly available by a federal, state, or local government entity. The term also does not include information that is encrypted, secured, or modified by any other method or technology that removes elements that personally identify an individual or that otherwise renders information unusable.

"*Third Party Agent*" means <u>an entity that has</u> <u>been contracted to maintain, store, or process</u> <u>personal information on behalf of a covered enti-</u> <u>ty or government entity</u>. Most covered entities generally are unaware of this concept. When confidential information sets are passed on to a third party for a legitimate purpose they, the sender, may still be responsible for maintaining the confidentiality of the data.

The reality is that for just about everyone who collects and maintains PII (Personally Identifiable Information) on others, he or she is required to take reasonable measures to protect the data. In addition, third-party entities that obtain and hold confidential information have the same obligation when the information has legitimately transferred to them.

Requirements for Data Security

The entire second section of FS 501.171 consists of a very brief general statement: *"Each covered entity, governmental entity or third-party agent shall take reasonable measures to protect and secure data in electronic form containing personal information."*

We'll outline what this very brief section might mean for you.

Disclaimer: The author of this report is an information security specialist, not an attorney. The opinions contained in this report should not be construed as legal advice. The reader should consult with a licensed attorney if legal counsel is required relative to the Statute.

There are a number of broad computer security standards that can be referenced when determining what might be considered "reasonable measures" to protect PII. One is the ISO 27000 series on information security. It is extensive and has a number of subsections. Others include COBIT, FISMA and a more recent guide produced by the NIST and commonly known as the Cyber Security Framework. None has the force of law. However, it is fair to state that most of them have the possibility of meeting the "reasonable measures" test.

We'll focus on the ISO 27002, when considering the range of what it might take for a covered entity to meet the test of taking 'reasonable measures to protect and secure data in electronic form'.

A topical list of standards and controls follows. It's is based on ISO 27002. Developing processes and procedures for each item would go a long way toward meeting the test of "reasonable care" with regard to handling PII:

1. Information Security Policies

2. Corporate Management of Information Security as a Business Process
3. Personnel Security Management
4. Organizational Asset Management
5. Information Access Management
6. Cryptography Policy Management
7. Physical Security Management
8. Operational Security Management
9. Network Security Management
10. System Security Management
11. Supplier Relationship Management
12. Security Incident Management
13. Security Continuity Management
14. Security Compliance Management

The International Standards Organization publishes the ISO 27000 information security series. The controls are recognized globally. The standards and suggestions are very detailed and comprehensive.

An organization that implemented ISO 27002 would have a very strong foundation for protecting against cyber intrusions, although it is well understood that there isn't anything such as "perfect security". In the author's opinion, however, an organization which has fully implemented the ISO 27002 standard would be deemed as having taken "reasonable measures" to secure its information infrastrucature.

We will discuss a number of the security standards later in this publication.

Notice to Department of Security Breach

The concern over a security breach relates to the fact that the personal and confidential information of an individual can be used to steal that person's digital identity. A malicious attacker or criminal organization could use a victim's private data to steal money from a bank or to open new lines of credit and make unauthorized purchases. There could be far reaching consequences for data breaches.

FS 501.171 is fairly explicit concerning what is required if an organization meeting certain criteria suffers a data breach of personally identifiable information.

A covered entity is required to notify the Department of Legal Affairs of any information security breach that affects more than 500 people in the State of Florida. The law makes reference to a requirement that an unauthorized disclosure be reported as "expeditiously as practicable in writing" within 30 days after determining that a breach occurred or reason to believe that a breach occurred.

The Statute states that a covered entity may receive 15 additional days to provide notice as required if good cause for delay is provided in writing to the Department within 30 days after determination or good reason to believe that a breach has occurred.

Specifications as to what information should be reported in writing to the Department are also in the Statute. Their essence is interpreted by the author below:

1. The organization against which the unauthorized access occurred must provide, in writing, a synopsis of the events that surrounded the data breach at the time notice is provided.

2. The report needs to reference the number of individuals who were or potentially have been affected by the data breach.

3. The entity must report any services related to the breach being offered or soon to be offered, without charge, to the individuals, and instructions on how to use such services.

For example, the entity might wish to provide a credit or fraud monitoring service to victims or those who could have been affected along with instructions on how to use the service.

4. A copy of the notice is required under the law or an explanation of the other actions taken pursuant to the law.

5. The name, address, telephone number and e-mail address of the employee or agent within the covered entity to contact for additional information about the breach.

The covered entity must also provide additional information upon its request:

a. A police report, incident report or forensics report
b. A copy of the policies in place regarding breaches
c. Steps that have been taken to rectify the breach

The Statute further specifies that the covered entity may provide additional information to the Department at any time. If a breach occurs in a state government agency the written notice to the Department requirement may be posted to the agency-managed website.

Notice to Individuals of Security Breach

Disclaimer: The author of this report is an information security specialist, not an attorney. The opinions contained

in this report should not be construed as legal advice. The reader should consult with a licensed attorney if legal counsel is required relative to the Statute.

Earlier it was mentioned that a covered entity is required to give notice to each individual in the State whose personal information was, or the covered entity reasonably believes to have been, accessed as a result of the breach.

a.) The notice must be made as expeditiously as possible and without an unreasonable delay, taking into account the time necessary to allow the covered entity to determine the nature and scope of the security breach to identify individuals affected by the breach, and to restore reasonable integrity of the data system that was breached. This should be done no later than 30 days after the determination of a breach or reason to believe that a breach occurred unless subject to a delay authorized by the law.

The law also has a further provision related to the responsibility for giving notice.

b.) If a federal, state or local law enforcement agency determines that giving notice interferes with a criminal investigation, the notice shall be delayed upon the written request of the law enforcement agencies for a specified period of time that the law enforcement agency determines is reasonably necessary.

c.) The Statute also states that notification to affected individuals is <u>not</u> required if, after an appropriate investigation and consultation with relevant federal, state, or local law enforcement, it is determined that the breach has not and will not likely result in identity theft or any other financial hardship to the individuals whose personal information has been accessed. Such a determination, however, needs to documented to the Department within 30 days after the determination and maintained for five (5) years.

d.) The law specifies the manner in which the required notification is to be given. Specifically, the notice may be:

1. A written notice from the covered entity may be sent to the mailing address of affected individuals

2. An e-mail sent to the electronic mail address of affected individuals

e.) The content of the notification shall include at a minimum:

1. The date, estimated date or estimated date range of the breach of security
2. A description of the personal information that was accessed or reasonably believed to have been accessed as a part of the breach of security

f.) The law provides for an alternative notification method if the cost of such notification exceeds $250,000, if the number of individuals exceeds 500,000 persons or if the covered entity doesn't have the e-mail address or mailing address for the affected individuals.   Substitute notifications shall include the following:

    1. A conspicuous notification on the website of the covered entity
    2. Notice in print and to broadcast media, including major media in urban and rural areas where the affected individual resides

Notice to Credit Reporting Agencies

If the covered entity is required to give notice to more than 1,000 individuals at a single time, the covered entity is required to notify all consumer reporting agencies that compile and maintain files on consumers on a nationwide basis, as defined in the Fair Credit Reporting Act.   The notice must include information about the timing, distribution and content.

Notice by Third-Party Agents; Duties of Third-Party Agents; Notice by Agents

Disclaimer: The author of this report is an information security specialist, not an attorney. The opinions contained in this report should not be construed as legal advice. The reader should consult with a licensed attorney if legal counsel is required relative to the Statute.

The Statute is explicit. If a breach of security occurs in a system that is maintained by a third-party agent, the third-party agent shall notify the *covered entity* of the breach of security as quickly as possible but no later than 10 days following the date of the breach or when it is believed that the breach took place.

The covered entity, in turn, is responsible for providing all of the required notices under the Statute upon being informed by the third-party agent that a security breach has occurred or is believed to have occurred. The third-party agent is also required to provide the covered entity with all of the information that is needed to comply with the provisions of the law.

The third-party agent may provide notice as required by law on behalf of the covered entity; however, an agent's failure to provide proper notice shall be deemed a violation of the requirements of the law on the part of the covered entity.

Annual Report

The Statute also requires that by February 1 of each year, the Department shall submit a report to the President of the Florida's State Senate and Speaker of the House of Representatives relating to breaches of security by governmental entities or third-party agencies of governmental entities in the preceding year along with recommendations for security improvements. Government entities that have violated any of the applicable requirements in the preceding year shall be identified.

Requirements for Disposal of Customer Records

When customer records are no longer to be retained, the law requires that covered entities or third-party agents take all reasonable measures to dispose, or arrange for the disposal of customer records that contain personal information within its custody being held. Such disposal is described as shredding, erasing or otherwise involving modifying the personal information in the records so as to make it unreadable or undecipherable through any means.

Enforcement

Disclaimer: The author of this report is an information security specialist, not an attorney. The opinions contained in this report should not be construed as legal advice. The

reader should consult with a licensed attorney if legal counsel is required relative to the Statute.

The law states that any violation of the provisions shall be considered to be an unfair or deceptive trade practice against the covered entity or third-party agent. The Statute provides for civil penalties for the following:

1. In the amount of $1,000 for each day up to the first 30 days following any violation of the law and then, thereafter, $50,000 for each subsequent 30-day period or portion thereof for up to 180 days

2. If the violation continues after 180 days, an amount not to exceed $500,000

Further, the civil penalties for failure to notify apply per breach and not per individual affected by the breach.

No Private Cause for Action

The law explicitly states the Statute doesn't establish a private cause of action.

Public Records Exemption

Disclaimer: The author of this report is an information security specialist, not an attorney. The opinions contained

in this report should not be construed as legal advice. The reader should consult with a licensed attorney if legal counsel is required relative to the Statute.

The Statute states that all of the information collected by the Department that is related to the investigation or law enforcement agency is confidential and exempt from s. 119.07(1) and s.24(a), Art. I of the State Constitution or until such time as the investigation is complete or ceases to be active. Further, that the Statute shall be construed as being in conformity with 119.071(2)(c).

Interestingly, during an investigation, the Department given certain conditions can disclose information. They include:

1. To further the Department's official duties and responsibilities

2. If the Department believes that such release of records would assist in notifying the public or locating and identifying people that the Department believes to be victims of the breach, improper disposal or exposure of confidential records

3. To give to another government entity to further its official duties and responsibilities

The Statute does state, however, that when the investigation is complete the following information received by the Department shall remain confidential and exempt from 2. 199.07(1) and s.24(a), Art I of the State Constitution:

1. All information to which public records ex-emptions applies
2. Personal information
3. A computer forensic report
4. Any information that would reveal a weak-ness in a covered entity's data security
5. Information that would reveal a covered entity's proprietary information

The term proprietary information means infor-mation that:

1. Is owned or controlled by the covered entity

2. Is intended to be private and treated by the covered entity as private because disclosure would have a negative effect on the covered enti-ty's business operations

3. Has not been disclosed except as required by law or agreement that provides that the information will not be released to the public

4. Is not publicly available or otherwise readi-ly decipherable through proper means from another source(s) in the same configuration as received by the Department

5. Also, trade secrets as defined in s.688.002 and competitive interest, the disclosure of which would impair the competitive business of the covered entity who is the subject of the information

The Statute closes with a statement that the law is subject to the Open Government Sunset Review Act in accordance with status and will stand repealed in October of 2019 unless reviewed and saved by the Legislature.

Summary

Most people use electronic computing devices in their business. Doing so means that they are operating in an asymmetric threat environment. Threats can emerge from any source. Organized crime, competitors, crackers and others are constantly searching for ways to intrude upon unauthorized information assets.

Business owners in Florida must now assess how the 2014 law (501.171), which relates to the security for the confidential personal information, is going to affect operations. The law mainly addresses who and what information is covered. The Statute is explicit about the responsibilities of what is known as a "covered entity". Reporting requirements are very detailed and include an explanation of civil fines.

The implications of Florida's 501.171 are extensive. The onus is now squarely on business
owners who are collecting, processing and utiliz-
ing personal information.

Clearly, Florida has many covered entities that
must be in sync with the provisions of the law.
Organizations, therefore, must have processes
and procedures in place so that they can comply.
Many don't.

A business would need to make information security a priority and think of it as a business
process. Doing anything less might prove to be
negligent in today's world.

How Can You Improve Information Security and Prevent Unauthorized Disclosures?

Disclaimer: The author of this report is an information security specialist, not an attorney. The opinions contained in this report should not be construed as legal advice. The reader should consult with a licensed attorney if legal counsel is required relative to the Statute.

Florida's statute, 501.171, relates to confidential personal information and makes reference to a couple of key expressions. One is located in the definition's section under "REQUIREMENTS FOR DATA SECURITY", – *"Each covered entity, governmental entity, or third-party agent shall take reasonable measures to protect and secure data in electronic form containing personal information."* The second expression appears again in the section entitled REQUIREMENTS FOR DISPOSAL OF CUSTOMER RECORDS – *"Each covered entity or third-party agent shall take all reasonable measures to dispose, or arrange for the disposal, of customer records containing personal information within its custody or control when the records are no longer to be retained. Such disposal shall involve shredding, erasing, or otherwise modifying the personal information in the records to make it unreadable or undecipherable through any means."*

An information security specialist would interpret the wording to be all-inclusive. That is, reasonable measures must be taken by all organizations to whom the law applies to protect the information throughout its life cycle. That's a tall order.

What can an organization do? How does a covered entity assure that it can meet the test of having taken *all reasonable measures*? The remainder of this section shall be devoted to answering these two questions.

a.) Information Security Policy

Does your organization or business have an information security policy? Do you have an inventory of all your information assets? The most basic of *reasonable measures* would likely be acknowledging that your organization is addressing the management of information security as a business process. If you are operating without one you should take steps to immediately establish a policy.

The depth and breadth of your information security policies is going to vary depending upon your organization's size and resources. Bear in mind, however, that an employer or manager can't expect the people in your company to be naturally aware of security if the company fails to acknowledge security as a business process, much like the manufacturing, transportation, finance or personnel functions.

Following information security best practices should be a part of everyday business life. For example, all new hires should be vetted as to their worthiness to handle confidential information prior to becoming employees. Another example of a security practice would be a policy to automatically remove network privileges for people who leave the employment of the organization.

An information security policy needs the support of top management, the Board or owner of the business. Employees will notice the lack of seriousness if the organization's leadership treats the information security policy as just another box to check off.

One startling fact that elevates the importance of information security is the simple fact that when an employee logs on to a computer system, more often than not, he or she is entering the interconnected world of the Internet. In that environment, if something can go wrong, it will.

b.) Inventory All Information Assets

Every one of your organization's information assets (documents, hardware, software, computers, etc.) should be inventoried. You must list every set of records and resources used to process your company's data.

Otherwise the consequence are quite clear. If you don't know what assets you have, how can you protect them?

An information security specialist can assist you in the process of gathering the details that would be needed to develop and implement a robust information security program to protect against an unauthorized intrusion.

c.) Classify All Information Assets

All of the assets that are identified in the inventory should be classified as to how critical they are to the company's operations. A publicly accessible website, for example, would be less important than confidential drawings of the organization's newest product.

A number of methods could be used to rank-order the confidentiality of information. The advantage would help management to better allocate their limited resources for security. One such classification system might appear as shown below:

Critical – The information is so confidential that its disclosure could cause serious damage to the organization

Restricted – Highly confidential information with limited distribution. Data is subject to compliance rules

Internal - Information that should be retained within the business

Public – Information that is regularly made available to the public

There are other classification structures. The point is that information assets are classified based upon their criticality to business operations.

d.) Deploy Logical and Physical Access Controls

The information infrastructure is owned by the organization. Management must exercise control over who can use it and how. End-users are without the right to determine the manner in which they interact with networks, computers, mobile and other electronic devices.

The owners of the infrastructure must control the physical and logical access to each component of the information system. Otherwise the system is already guaranteed to be vulnerable.

Physical access control means that controls are in place to keep unauthorized individuals from getting close to information assets. That type of control would include logging in visitors to the office and keeping information assets behind locked doors. A "Visitor" badge might be appropriate.

Physical access can also be controlled by wiring the building in a manner that puts layers of defense between an intruder's attempts to gain access and the device itself. For example, a network server shouldn't be located in the front of the building in a more public space such as where workers are located in cubicles.

Wireless communications in a building can also be limited. Many "Hot Spots" can physically adjust their broadcast range. Attention needs to paid to the zones into which electronic signals reach. Crackers and hackers have been known to access electronic signals from a company's parking lot. Anything that can reduce the attack surface with which a cyber criminal has to work should be done.

Logical access to computers is somewhat different. It uses software to authorize users to electronic space. There are three main types of logical access controls. One is using complex passwords. Another is using biometrics such as a fingerprint or retina scan. The third is the use of a token. Each method of authentication relates to something the user is, has or knows. An attempt to access digital resources is logically tested to determine if the user is authorized.

Security specialists will recommend that ideally all three methods of authentication should be implemented (something the user knows, something the user is or something the user has).

e.) Use Network Firewalls and Intrusion Detection Devices

Think of a firewall as facing the Internet and being a gateway into a network or your computer.

Firewalls come in two varieties: one is hardware and the other is software. The hardware version of a firewall can be "programmed" to accept only certain Internet addresses and to exclude others. Hardware firewalls are typically associated with networks. A firewall device can help with blocking unauthorized intrusions. The second variety of firewall uses software to examine inbound and outbound data from the Internet. This type is less robust but useful for individual, free-standing computers.

The government and other organizations keep up with the latest cyber attacks and IP addresses that are known to be used by criminals. These toxic Internet addresses can be blocked from accessing your information infrastructure.

Certain Internet services can also be disabled and blocked. The use of a firewall is considered to be a security best practice.

f.) Secure the Work Space

Desktop computers, workstations, printers and all other electronic data processing devices should only be accessible to authorized users. The computer terminals or workstations should be locked when the worker takes a break. Workstations should have special screens installed on the monitors that would make it more difficult for bystanders to read what is on the screen.

Any removable media should be taken out and secured on workstations when authorized users leave the work space. Any papers or confidential information should be removed from the tops of desks. Office doors to work spaces should be closed and locked, even if the workers has only left briefly.

g.) Data in Transit Should be Protected

Data that is on the move needs to be protected from prying eyes or malicious crackers. One way of doing so is to use a Virtual Private Network or VPN. The confidentiality and integrity of information can be maintained by using one. A VPN uses publicly switched telephone lines and encryption to protect information.

Data and information with which an organization works is protected from intrusions, theft and alterations when being transmitted over a VPN. Conducting business using a VPN makes it possible to maintain any communications you might have.

h.) Manage Mobile Devices

An information security plan should have policies and procedures in place for mobile devices.

People frequently work while on the road traveling. Research indicates that more than 60% of U.S. employees use a smart phone to connect to company networks. The use of laptops and smart phones is nearly pervasive.

The vulnerabilities associated with mobile devices are extensive. Among the issues is whether or not employees bring their own device or are forced to use a company owned phone. The business data stored on mobile devices is usually highly sensitive and if lost, could cause real trouble for a business or organization. The jury is in – increased use of mobile devices upon which to conduct business has had a negative impact on the security of information as well as compliance. The number of mobile devices infected with malware increased more than 25% in one recent year.

Personally identifiable information being held on customers, for example, could be compromised. Other sensitive data could be exposed. Compliance issues are very broad. Included in the threat mix are "apps" that may be considered malware. A cyber criminal could gain access to such data through wireless hot spots or the outright theft of the portable device or through cloud storage.

What are the solutions? Some experts believe that "single-sign-on" access and multi-factored authentication would be the answer. Using only company owned smart phones and disallowing the download of apps from any source other than those that are approved is a security best practice. Sensitive information should be encrypted. Lost or stolen devices should have the capability of being wiped cleaned remotely.

i.) Develop an Incident or Data Breach Response Plan

Organizations need to be aware of a security breach as soon as possible. However, maintaining business continuity is the first priority. Once the continuance of business operations is assured, an incident response plan (which should already be in place), needs to be put into action. The importance of this process can't be over emphasized. The damage caused by an intrusion must be contained. The amount of damage needs to be assessed. Forensic evidence must be preserved and continuing to operate the business is a top priority.

The scope of what was lost, altered or damaged as a result of an intrusion, must be determined. Any compliance issues must be handled appropriately (such as making mandatory notifications according to FS 501.171).

Areas of responsibility must be clearly defined for each individual within the organization. Each employee needs to follow through on his or her responsibilities.

After assuring business continuity the organization needs to understand how the successful attack occurred. The defenses of the information system would need to be strengthened. One of the objectives would be to prevent additional attacks by codifying "lessons learned".

Policies and procedures that need to be modified must be adopted to make the system's information security more robust. Perpetrators of the intrusion need to be prosecuted if at all possible and properly preserving evidence so that it stands up in court is essential.

A wise information infrastructure owner must seriously consider following the controls and guidelines associated with a well-understood global standard such as the ISO 27000.

j.) Back-up and Business Continuity Plan

The idea of having redundancy built into an information infrastructure is crucial so that data can be restored. There are numerous ways in which back-up can be done. In all cases pre-planning is essential. The point and purpose of the back-up is so that business operations can continue.

A business continuity plan outlines, in a systematic manner, what should be done to preserve the continuing operations of the organization. Such a plan is a detailed and in-depth outline of how the organization would be saved in the event of a natural disaster, a cyber attack or Act of God.

Survival of the organization would likely depend upon the restoration of the company's software. A duplicate information infrastructure, located on a separate site, is typically part of a business continuity plan.

k.) Data, Media and Hardware Destruction

Very few people realize that when computer media is deleted from a hard drive, for example, an expert can still recover it. Information infrastructure owners must be aware that all computers, hard-drives, tapes, CDs and equipment need to be appropriately destroyed. Otherwise, any media that falls into the hands of nefarious individuals can be accessed.

An organization should make the processes and procedures for data destruction clear. There are commercial organizations that specialize in the destruction of electronic media. It is defined as any electronically generated storage that is used to record information including, but not limited to hard drives, magnetic tapes, compact disks, video tapes, audio tapes, and removable storage such as floppy and zip disks.

l.) Design a Security Awareness Program

Every organization should have an information security awareness program and it needs to be outlined in the company's policies and procedures.

New hires should receive computer security awareness training on a routine basis during their term of employment. Constant reinforcement of security best practices is highly recommended. Each new-hire should have to sign off on his or her responsibilities relative to the confidential information that is handled.

Workers and existing management should be made aware of the threats and vulnerabilities that the organization faces. For example, everyone should be aware of the social engineering techniques that are used to compromise network security for the purpose of unauthorized disclosure.

Each employee should be educated on how to maintain a safe work place and should know how to handle confidential information. Considerations include:

1. What is personally identifiable information?
2. How do you properly process and work with confidential information?
3. What is a risk?
4. What is social engineering?
5. What are the information security policies about which you should be aware?
6. What is involved in maintaining good workplace security practices?
7. Does everyone know how to properly handle stored information?

8.   What is considered to be appropriate use of the organization's information assets?

9.   How must confidential information be created, stored and destroyed?

10.   What are the threats that our organization faces?

11.   What are the company's mobile device policies?

12.   What are the "Do's" and "Don't's" of using the Internet?

Summary

Florida's information privacy Statute 501.171 requires that organizations must take reasonable measures to handle confidential information. The law doesn't precisely dictate, however, the details of what information policies and procedures should be.

There are a number of information security controls and standards, none of which carry the force of law. However, many are considered to be very robust security models.

Organizations must have an information security policy. Otherwise, guidance from management is absent. Meeting the test of "reasonableness" under the Statute would be challenging if the organization failed to address the topic in its official operating policies.

The idea of inventorying information assets is also basic. How could you protect information assets that you are holding if you are without a list of what you possess? Information assets should be classified as to their criticality. Doing so is one way to determine where limited assets should be deployed.

There are numerous technical and non-technical means for limiting risk. Acknowledging threats and vulnerabilities faced by the organization is a beginning and the right step toward mitigating risks that could be extremely harmful to a company's existence.